Every boy and girl has heard of Nelson, one of the bravest fighting sailors England has ever known. Here is the story of his life, from his first boyhood voyage to his last great victory at Trafalgar.

Acknowledgment
The painting of *HMS Victory* on the front endpaper is by Monamy Swain, and is reproduced by permission of the National Maritime Museum, Greenwich.

Nelson

written and illustrated
by FRANK HUMPHRIS

Ladybird Books Loughborough

When the news of Nelson's death at Trafalgar reached England, a deep sense of grief and loss was felt throughout the country. The whole of England mourned the death of a great national hero. In the usually noisy dockside taverns, sailors were silent or talked only in low tones. Many had tears in their eyes.

Seven royal dukes attended the great state funeral and the coffin was borne by no less than six admirals, while many thousands of people lined the route to the last resting place in St Paul's Cathedral.

What was there about Nelson that inspired such great emotion in the hearts of the English people?

First, the time in which he lived was one of great uncertainty and danger for this country. England was under threat of invasion by the French. Almost the whole of Europe had fallen to the victorious armies of Napoleon Bonaparte. Everywhere on land they seemed unbeatable and only at sea had the French met their match. And it was Nelson who time and again had defeated them in a series of brilliant naval battles. Finally, at Trafalgar, the combined fleets of France and Spain had been almost completely destroyed, removing once and for all Napoleon's chance of invading England.

Nelson's life as a sailor began at an early age. He was only twelve years old when he left his boyhood home to become a midshipman on board his uncle's ship, the *Raisonnable*. It had 64 guns and lay at Chatham. When his uncle was transferred to the guardship *Triumph* (also based at Chatham), he took his nephew with him.

Nelson joins his uncle's ship

Horatio Nelson was born in 1758, the fifth son of the Reverend Edmund Nelson, the rector of Burnham Thorpe in Norfolk.

The little boy was lucky to have an uncle who was captain of a ship in the Royal Navy, for without influence his life would have been extremely hard in a ship of that time. One of the first things his uncle did was to send Horatio on a long voyage to the West Indies in a merchant ship. This was to give him some sea-going experience, which he would not get on a harbour ship such as the *Triumph*.

On his return from this voyage, he was put in command of the ship's boats sailing between the Nore and the Pool of London. He was just fourteen years old.

Mastering the tricky skills of navigation in a tidal estuary was good training in practical seamanship for the young midshipman.

Next he was allowed to join an expedition to the Arctic, serving as coxwain of the captain's gig. It was said that during this voyage he had one of his first adventures, for while the ships were trapped in the ice, he encountered a polar bear and, boy-like, decided to try to obtain the skin as a trophy. Unfortunately, his musket misfired and he prepared to rush forward and attack the great animal with the butt of his gun.

Luckily his plight was seen, and a shot was fired from the ship. The bear lumbered off and young Horatio returned saying he had only wanted to get the skin for his father.

Nelson's next voyage was to the East Indies in the 20 gun ship, *Seahorse*, but while among the islands he caught a tropical fever and was invalided home.

He was very ill and cared little whether he lived or died. As he himself said, 'I almost wished myself overboard. But a sudden glow of patriotism was kindled within me. Well then, I exclaimed, I will be a hero, and confiding in Providence I will brave every danger.' Nelson lived up to that resolve to the end of his life.

As soon as he was fit again he was posted to a ship sailing to the West Indies. He was now eighteen and in April, 1777, having served six years at sea, at least two of them as a midshipman in the Royal Navy, he was made a lieutenant.

His captain was William Locker, a distinguished officer who became a great friend of the young lieutenant. It was his advice to 'Lay a Frenchman close and you will beat him' that Nelson later adopted as his fighting signal.

There is no doubt that Nelson's enthusiasm, courage, and professional competence, as well as his charm of manner, marked him out as an exceptional young officer.

After service with Captain Locker, he was transferred to the flagship of the Commander in Chief and on 11th June, 1779 was promoted to post-captain.

He was four months short of his 21st birthday.

A captain at nearly 21

As captain of a frigate, Nelson took a distinguished part in the amphibious attack against Spanish possessions in Central America. He led his men up the river in small boats, but it was the time of the tropical rains and the troops were ill-equipped for jungle warfare. Yellow fever took its toll. Out of two hundred men only ten survived. Nelson himself was very ill indeed, and once again, found himself back in England to recover his health.

Upon his return to sea he served first in North America, then was ordered once more to the West Indies. This was a difficult time for Nelson. His task was to prevent the islanders trading with the former colonists of the now independent United States of America as if

Nelson commands a frigate in the West Indies

10

they were still British subjects. In fact the trade was beneficial to both countries, and, in trying to carry out the letter of the law, Nelson became unpopular with nearly everyone.

His only friends ashore were Mr Herbert of the island of Nevis and his niece, Mrs Frances Nesbit, a young widow with a five year old son. The lonely young captain, starved of feminine company, fell in love and after a two year courtship the two were married in 1787.

Shortly afterwards the Nelsons sailed for England where, as peace had been proclaimed, the ship was paid off and her captain placed on reduced pay of £50 per year.

The six years of peace that followed were spent by Nelson and his family at the parsonage in Norfolk. Then on the outbreak of war with France in 1793 he was given command of the *Agamemnon*, a 64 gun ship of the line, and ordered to join the Mediterranean fleet.

The *Agamemnon* was a two-decker mounting 32 guns on each side, and powerful enough to fight with bigger ships in the line of battle. It was Nelson's first big ship.

One of his first duties in the Mediterranean was to sail to Naples, then an independent state, to ask for assistance against the French. There he met for the first time the British Ambassador, Sir William Hamilton and his wife, the beautiful Lady Hamilton. She was to play an important part in his later life.

Meanwhile, Britain was in urgent need of a Mediterranean base and harbours for her ships, and it was decided to capture the island of Corsica then held by the French.

Nelson was prominent in the attacks on their fortifications and it was while he was supervising a battery of guns at Calvi that a French cannonball struck the ground nearby. Splinters of stone were driven up into his face and he lost the sight of his right eye.

To be blinded in one eye was a hard blow to the ambitious young sea captain, but it did not deter Nelson for long.

Early the following year a French fleet of seventeen ships ventured out of the port of Toulon with the intention of recapturing Corsica. But at sight of the fourteen British ships on the horizon, the French put about to return to the safety of Toulon. In the manoeuvre, one of their largest ships, the *Ça Ira*, collided with another vessel and was partially dismasted.

A British frigate, not far away, sailed into attack but was driven off by two large French ships that then took the *Ça Ira* in tow. Nelson, in the fast sailing *Agamemnon*, was already far ahead of the rest of the British fleet, and as he came up to the dismasted Frenchman he opened fire.

Handling his ship with great skill so as to avoid the return fire of the enemy ship, he poured broadside after broadside into her. Finally, with over four hundred dead, she struck her colours and surrendered. One other ship was captured, but the rest of the French fleet escaped.

This was Nelson's first fleet action and his daring and success established his reputation as a fighting captain.

A new Commander in Chief was now appointed to the Mediterranean fleet. He was Admiral Sir John Jervis, a man after Nelson's own heart. Quick to recognise merit, it was he who promoted the young captain to the rank of commodore.

The war was going badly for Britain, and with Spain throwing in her lot with Napoleon, the greatly outnumbered British fleet had to leave the Mediterranean.

The capture of the Ça Ira

Nelson, who had remained behind to help in the evacuation of Elba, was sailing to rejoin the main fleet in the Atlantic when the ship ran into fog. Through the swirling mist the British sailors could see the dim outlines of other ships, but the voices that came over the water were speaking — Spanish!

The Spaniards had left harbour and were sailing to join the French fleet at Brest. Fortunately, Nelson managed to sail completely through them without being detected, and joined Jervis in time for the forthcoming battle.

The Spanish fleet of twenty seven ships was in two groups, and Jervis, with only fifteen ships, knew he must adopt a different plan from the usual one of sailing in parallel lines exchanging broadsides with the enemy. He determined to make for the gap between the two Spanish squadrons, split their fleet, and overwhelm the first half before the second half arrived.

Then occurred one of the most remarkable actions in the history of naval warfare. Nelson, in the 74 gun ship, *Captain*, lay to the rear of the British line and realised that the two sections of the Spanish fleet would be united before the British plan could operate successfully.

He decided on a daring and highly unconventional manoeuvre. Without orders and risking court-martial and disgrace, he turned out of the battle line, and sailed the *Captain* across the bows of the advancing Spanish. Immediately the ship became the target for the Spanish gunners. The fore topmast went overboard and the wheel was shot away, but skilfully Nelson managed to manoeuvre his vessel into the 80 gun *San Nicolas*, and the two ships became closely locked together.

With drawn sword Nelson led the boarding party on to the deck of the larger ship which, after a short sharp fight, surrendered.

In the smoke and confusion another enemy ship, the huge 112 gun *San Josef*, had drifted up to the other side of the *San Nicolas*. No sooner had the first ship surrendered than the boarding party found themselves under fire from the *San Josef*.

Shouting 'Westminster Abbey or glorious victory,' Nelson scrambled aboard the *San Josef*. He and his men attacked with such fury that the Spanish captain promptly surrendered. It was an astounding victory. Two great enemy ships, both larger than his own, had been captured by Nelson and the men of the *Agamemnon*.

Fighting aboard the San Josef

18

At home Nelson's name was on everyone's lips. He was the toast of London, and in recognition of his achievements was knighted and promoted to rear admiral. But not every action of his was equally successful.

In July of 1797 he went on an ill-advised expedition to try to capture a Spanish treasure ship sheltering at the Spanish island of Teneriffe. Nelson had about eleven hundred men to pit against eight thousand Spanish troops, and the British faced massive gunfire from the fortress of Santa Cruz.

Nelson took part in the final attack in defiance of orders not to set foot ashore. During the fighting his right arm was so badly shattered by grapeshot that it had to be amputated. There followed many months ashore as he was nursed back to health by his wife. It was a period of intense depression.

He felt that his career was ended: 'A left-handed admiral will never again be considered ... I am become a burden to my friends and useless to my country.'

The authorities had other ideas however. In March, 1798 he was posted to the Mediterranean in response to the requests of his Commander in Chief, Admiral Jervis, now Earl St Vincent. His task was to investigate the large concentrations of troops and ships that Napoleon was assembling in the Mediterranean ports of France and northern Italy, but a heavy storm dismasted Nelson's *Vanguard* and allowed the French fleet to slip away unobserved. The vital question was – in which direction were they heading?

Nelson loses an arm at Teneriffe

21

The hunt for the French fleet was on! News reached Nelson that Napoleon's armada was seen heading eastward off the island of Sicily, and by an inspired guess he decided that they were making for Egypt.

Napoleon's imaginative scheme was to conquer Egypt and thus establish a base in the middle east from which the French could harass the British, and eventually drive them from India. It was an ambitious plan, in keeping with Napoleon's grandiose ideas of conquest.

The British ships made for Egypt at their best speed,

GOLIATH

FRENCH

DIAGRAM of the BATTLE of the NILE

The French ships are at anchor in Aboukir Bay.

The British ships are shown approaching the head of the French line and sailing round it to attack from the landward side.

and in so doing, by-passed the French who had stopped to secure the island of Malta as a supply base. Egypt was reached but to Nelson's bitter disappointment there was no sign of the enemy. He sailed on to search the coasts of Syria, Turkey and Greece, unaware that only a few hours after his departure the French sails had appeared off the Egyptian coast.

A month was wasted in fruitless searching before Nelson again returned to Egypt to find the French fleet at anchor in Aboukir Bay near Alexandria. The date was August 1st, 1798.

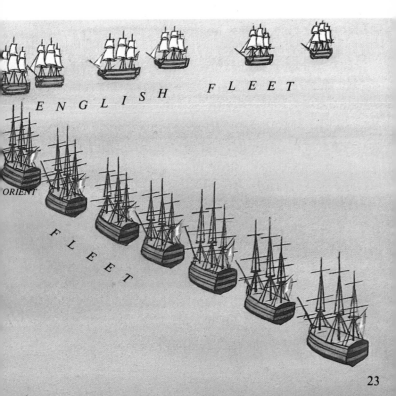

The French admiral had drawn up his ships into a seemingly impregnable position close to the shore, with their guns facing seaward.

It was evening and darkness was falling fast, but Nelson attacked at once. Braving the shallows inshore, Captain Foley in *Goliath* sailed round the end of the French line and attacked them in the rear. He was followed by other ships. The French, completely unprepared for this bold and unexpected action, were caught in the cross-fire.

In the gathering dark the scene was lit by the flashes from the guns. It was not long before the largest enemy ship, *L'Orient*, caught fire, and the flames spreading with fearful rapidity threw a lurid light over the scene. At 10.15 pm the flames reached the powder magazine, and with a tremendous explosion the ship blew up.

A British captain described the scene: 'An awful pause and death-like silence ensued, until the wreck of the masts and yards which had been carried to an immense height, fell down into the water and on neighbouring ships.'

Only four French ships escaped. Not only had Napoleon lost his fleet, but his army of some 5,000 men was now isolated in Egypt. It was the end of his dream of a middle-eastern empire. And it had shown to Europe, including England's wavering allies, that the conqueror was not unbeatable after all.

The L'Orient *blows up*

24

Nelson's fame resounded throughout Europe. George III elevated him to the peerage, the King of Naples created him Duke of Brontë and gave him a large (though penniless) estate in Sicily. The Sultan of Turkey presented him with a fabulous jewelled ornament, while a diamond-studded box containing his portrait came from the Tsar of Russia.

However, Nelson had not come through the battle unscathed. A flying piece of jagged metal had struck him on the forehead, cutting the flesh to the bone. It was a painful though not dangerous wound.

After the battle the British fleet made for Naples for repairs and rest, where Nelson was invited to stay at the Embassy as guest of the Hamiltons.

Lady Hamilton was overcome when she saw Nelson again. The slight boyish figure of a few years ago now showed only too clearly the ravages of war. The jagged wound showed clearly on his forehead and the empty sleeve pinned to his coat told its own tragic story. As he returned her gaze with his one good eye, she went forward impulsively with arms outstretched ... It was the beginning of the great romance that was to link their names together for all time.

Nelson's presence encouraged the King of Naples to attack the French in the north of Italy, with disastrous results, and Nelson had to transport the Neapolitan court to Sicily. It was two years before he saw England again.

Sir William and Lady Hamilton meet Nelson

27

In spite of Britain's successes at sea, Napoleon dominated most of the continent of Europe, and Britain was left to carry on the war alone.

To make the most of our superior sea power it was therefore decided to place a blockade on the French coasts as far as possible, and stop all ships of whatever nationality from entering or leaving French ports.

This action prevented the neutral powers from trading with France, a fact which they resented. In consequence, Russia, Prussia, Denmark and Sweden formed an armed neutrality pact which would have operated against Britain's efforts to enforce the blockade.

28

The battle of Copenhagen, 1801

As Britain was at war with France, Spain and Holland it could have developed into a very dangerous situation, so a British fleet under Admiral Sir Hyde Parker, with Nelson as his second in command, was sent to seal off the Baltic.

It was planned to defeat the Danish fleet before the Russians and Prussians could come to their assistance. Parker was a cautious man however. Instead of attacking immediately, he sent representatives ashore to try to persuade the Danes to withdraw from the alliance. These negotiations failed, but while they were going on, the Danish fleet had time to concentrate its forces in a strong position off Copenhagen.

Admiral Parker put Nelson in charge of the ships of shallow draught to enable him to get in close, but it became clear to Nelson that there was no room for tactical manoeuvre, and that the forthcoming battle would be long and difficult.

The British squadron included twelve ships of the line but the battle began badly for them when three of the ships ran aground in shallow water. The other nine went on and anchored opposite the Danes, and the bombardment began.

Broadside followed broadside and soon the fleets were hidden in great clouds of smoke. The Danes had brought up several floating batteries to increase their fire power and as Nelson had foreseen, it was a hard pounding match. At one time, Parker, thinking that Nelson would be beaten, gave the signal for the ships to withdraw.

Nelson however was determined to fight on and when the message was brought to him, he put the telescope to his blind eye and exclaimed, 'I really do not see the signal.'

The battle continued for another hour before the Danes had had enough, and when Nelson saw this he sent a flag of truce with a message to the effect that the brave Danes were the brothers and should never be the enemies of the British.

It was a hard-fought victory, but one which received little public acclaim. Nevertheless, with a new Tzar on the throne of Russia, peace was soon concluded.

For a short time there was also peace with France, but Napoleon's restless ambitions made any permanent settlement unlikely. Nelson came home on the grounds of ill health and lived a quiet country life on an estate at Merton that he had purchased.

But it was not for long.

In 1803 hostilities broke out again, and Nelson, now Commander in Chief, hoisted his flag in the *Victory*. He sailed once more for the Mediterranean, where a large French fleet was located in the port of Toulon.

A long weary period of watching and waiting followed. For almost two years the British squadron cruised off the coast and Nelson was rarely out of his ship. At last the French fleet managed to break out, evade the

The French fleet is sighted off Cadiz

British and pass into the Atlantic. Other French and Spanish ships in various ports were also under instructions to put to sea, cross the Atlantic to the West Indies, and thus draw the British blockading forces away from Europe. They were then to unite in one great fleet and sail back to the English Channel in readiness for the French invasion of England.

However, Villeneuve's squadron was the only one that managed to escape, and it was chased by Nelson across the Atlantic and back again without, unfortunately, being sighted and brought to action. Eventually Villeneuve and his ships took refuge in the Spanish port of Cadiz, where they were found and blockaded.

33

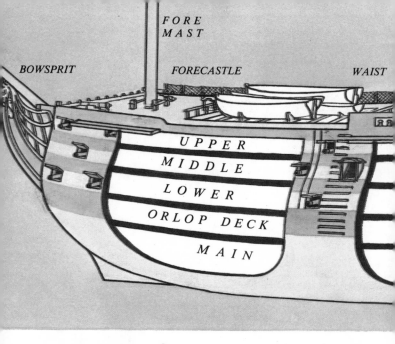

FORE MAST

BOWSPRIT   FORECASTLE   WAIST

UPPER

MIDDLE

LOWER

ORLOP DECK

MAIN

With the stage set for the final decisive battle, let us take a closer look at a ship of the period. A big three-decker like Nelson's flagship, the *Victory*, was a formidable fighting machine mounting over 100 guns and carrying a crew of some 850 officers and men.

By modern standards it was short and wide, being 226 ft 6 in in length and 52 ft 6 in wide. The main mast rose to a height of 215 ft from the keel. The main-yard — the longest spar in the ship — measured 102 ft 4 in in length and weighed six tons. Just above the main-yard was the main 'top', a kind of platform on which, during a battle, a group of musketeers would be stationed. From here they could fire down on the enemy's decks.

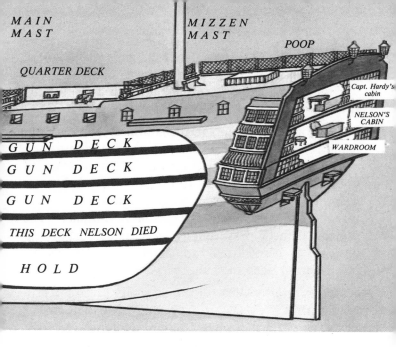

MAIN MAST — MIZZEN MAST — POOP — QUARTER DECK — Capt. Hardy's cabin — NELSON'S CABIN — WARDROOM — GUN DECK — GUN DECK — GUN DECK — THIS DECK NELSON DIED — HOLD

Each mast was fitted with one of these 'tops'. (It was a musketeer firing from the mizzen top of the *Redoubtable* who killed Nelson.)

The officers' living quarters were situated aft at the stern, the admiral having both a day cabin and a dining-room. By contrast the crew lived in overcrowded conditions on the gun-decks. They ate at tables slung between the guns, and slept in hammocks hanging from the deck beams. On the middle gun-deck was the galley, containing an iron stove on which the cooking was done for all 850 officers and crew.

The *Victory* is still in existence. It can be seen in Portsmouth dockyard looking exactly as it did at Trafalgar.

This sectional drawing shows the great depth of the *Victory*. There are no less than four main decks within the hull, with the quarter-deck and poop-deck forming two more. The hold is 21 ft 6 in deep.

The noise of the guns in the confined space was appalling and men wore hats or neckerchiefs tied over their ears. Many were deafened permanently. Those wounded in battle were taken below to the orlop deck below the waterline, where such crude surgery as was possible was carried on in the dimly-lit and noisome atmosphere. The only anaesthetic was rum. The surgeon's cabin and dispensary, carpenter's cabin, midshipmen's berths, powder magazines and cable tiers are also on this deck.

Below the orlop deck is the hold where stores and provisions for the voyage were carried. To give some idea of just a few of the many items and the quantities required, the list below gives the amount in tons.

Powder	35 tons	Water	300 tons
Shot	120 tons	Beef and pork	25/30 tons
Iron ballast	600 tons	Flour	10 tons
Biscuits	45 tons	Peas	15 tons
Beer	200 tons	Coal and charcoal	50 tons

As most of the provisions were carried in wooden barrels in a damp unventilated space, the condition of the food during a long period at sea can be imagined.

Efficient gunnery was the main key to the naval battles of the eighteenth century. Once the ships were in position the battle became a pounding match, each side trying to inflict the utmost damage to the enemy's ships and personnel. Much practice and training was needed to achieve this expertise.

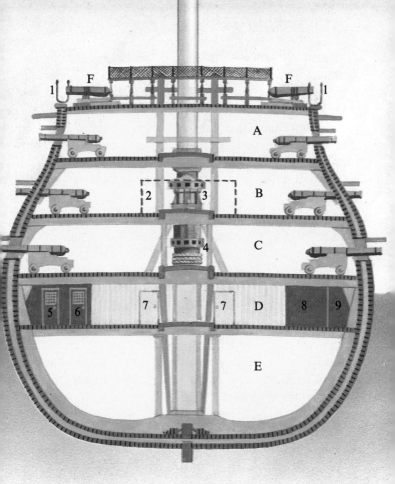

Upper Gun Deck with thirty two guns firing 12lb shot
Middle Gun Deck with thirty guns firing 24lb shot
Lower Gun Deck with thirty guns firing 32lb shot
Orlop Deck
Main Hold
Carronades. Short heavy guns firing 68lb shot

1 Brackets for Hammock Nettings (rolled sleeping hammocks were piled here to give protection)
2 Galley, Cooking Stove on brick floor
3 Capstan Head   4 Main Capstan
5 Dispensary   6 Surgeon's Cabin
7 Magazines for storing gunpowder charges
8 Cockpit, wounded were treated here
9 Carpenter's Walk, from which underwater damage was repaired

37

A crew of about fifteen men were responsible for handling a gun, first on the one side of the ship, then as the ship changed course, the opposite gun on the other side. The loading sequence was as follows: A cloth cartridge containing the gunpowder was loaded into the muzzle and rammed home. This was followed by a wad and then the shot of whatever type was being used, either ball, chain or canister, then a rope wad to hold all in place.

Next, the order was given to run the gun out and the men at the side ropes hauled away until the muzzle protruded beyond the gun-port. Priming powder was then poured into the vent and with the gun captain giving directions, the gun was aimed by two of the crew, training it to the right or left with handspikes, helped by the men on the side tackles.

If it was necessary to alter the elevation, the handspikes were again used to raise the breech, so that the second gun captain could adjust the huge wooden wedge upon which the breech of the gun rested. To depress the barrel, the wedge was pushed further in; to elevate the barrel it was pulled out, until the desired level was reached.

The gun was fired either by *slow match* (a length of loose hemp rope soaked in spirits of wine or a solution of saltpetre, which burned slowly and evenly) or by a flintlock mechanism attached to the breech. After each firing the barrel had to be swabbed out and any smouldering remains of the cartridge extracted by means of a 'worm' on the end of a rod.

The gun captain gives directions for the aiming of the gun. The men lever the gun round with handspikes.

A TYPICAL 32 POUNDER
Length: 9 ft 6 in
Weight: 2 tons 15½ cwt
Diameter of shot: 6.1 in

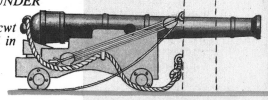

VARIOUS TYPES OF BAR, CHAIN, AND GRAPE SHOT

Bar and chain shot were designed for damaging enemy rigging, spars and sails.

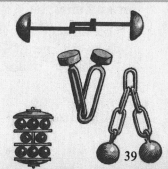

39

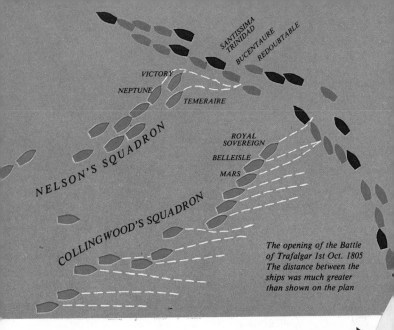

SANTISSIMA TRINIDAD
BUCENTAURE
REDOUBTABLE

VICTORY
NEPTUNE
TEMERAIRE

ROYAL SOVEREIGN
BELLEISLE
MARS

NELSON'S SQUADRON

COLLINGWOOD'S SQUADRON

The opening of the Battle of Trafalgar 1st Oct. 1805 The distance between the ships was much greater than shown on the plan

Gunnery diagram ➡

To use the guns to their best advantage, the ship had to be manoeuvred into the right position. This meant with the side towards the enemy so that the full broadside could be used. Only the two carronades on the forecastle could be manoeuvred to fire in a forward direction.

The diagram shows how a ship sailing towards the enemy line, would, for a time, be a target unable to reply until the breakthrough, when the full effect of the broadsides tearing through the length of the opposing vessels would be devastating.

40

BRITISH

FRENCH

SPANISH

Nelson's plan for the battle of Trafalgar

The British ships are approaching in two columns, with the intention of splitting and disorganising the French line.

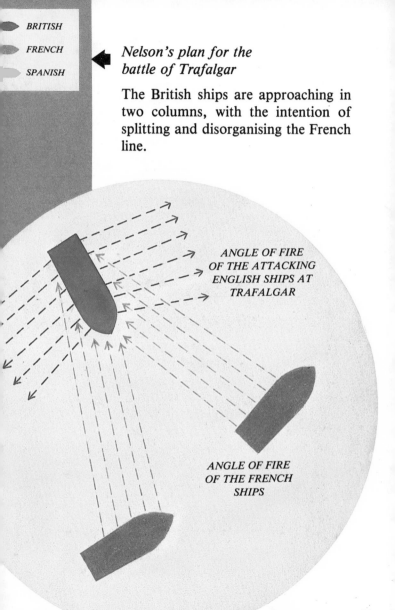

ANGLE OF FIRE OF THE ATTACKING ENGLISH SHIPS AT TRAFALGAR

ANGLE OF FIRE OF THE FRENCH SHIPS

After a harrowing two years of continuous service at sea and the fruitless chase across the Atlantic and back, Nelson's squadron joined Admiral Collingwood's stationed off southern Spain. Nelson himself, dispirited at the failure to bring the enemy to battle, returned in the *Victory* to England, to await developments.

It was to be his last three weeks in England.

On 1st September, Captain Blackwood of the frigate *Euryalus* arrived in England with the news of Villeneuve's arrival at Cadiz, and on 14th September, Nelson sailed from Portsmouth in the *Victory* to join Collingwood's blockading force off Cadiz on the 28th. Over the horizon the masts of the combined fleets of France and Spain could be seen in the harbour.

Nelson was welcomed by the British fleet with great enthusiasm. Immediately plans were drawn up for the impending battle – plans which Nelson described in a letter to Lady Hamilton as 'The Nelson touch which *we* say is warranted never to fail.'

Basically (as shown on pages 40-41), the British planned to sail for the enemy's line in two main columns, break through about one third of the way down from the leading ships, and concentrate the superior fire power on the rear two thirds. The idea was bold, original and guaranteed to confuse the enemy.

Meanwhile, Napoleon had ordered the French and Spanish fleets to put to sea and to fight if necessary, and Villeneuve had no option but to obey.

Nelson leaves England for the last time

The morning of October 21st, 1805 dawned fine but misty. From the topmost yards of the *Victory*, the combined French and Spanish fleet of thirty five ships could be seen sailing in a southerly direction a few miles westward of Cape Trafalgar.

In accordance with Nelson's battle plan, the British fleet of twenty seven ships manoeuvred into position and bore down on the enemy in two columns, one led by Nelson, the other by Admiral Collingwood. The wind was light and variable from the west. Progress was slow.

On board the ships, drums beat the call to action, the gun-port lids were raised and the guns loaded and run out, brine tubs for the slow matches used in firing the

The start of the battle of Trafalgar

guns were placed in position, the decks were sanded, ammunition was brought from below and all around was the activity and preparation for a major sea battle. It was at this time that Nelson hoisted the famous signal: 'England expects that every man will do his duty.'

As the British ships approached head on, it was obvious that they would come under heavy fire before they could break through the enemy line and bring their own broadsides into action. The *Victory* was hit again and again. She suffered considerable damage to the rigging and many casualties before she glided between the *Bucentaure* and the *Redoubtable,* pouring a devastating broadside into the stern windows of the former as she passed, and raking the ship from end to end.

BATTLE OF TRAFALGAR

47

The French 74 gun *Redoubtable,* sailing close astern of the *Bucentaure,* was struck by the bows of the *Victory*. She swung to starboard, and the two ships became locked together by the entangled rigging.

By this time the *Victory* had lost both fore and mizzen topmasts and main topgallant mast. On deck, marines were lined up at the hammock nettings firing point blank at their opponents. The 68 lb carronades on the forecastle caused appalling havoc to the French boarding parties forming to attack, while down below the heavy guns were firing broadside after broadside, not a shot of which could miss at such short range.

Meanwhile, other ships following the *Victory* had also surged through the French line, and having raked the

nearest ship as they passed were ranging alongside the enemy vessels. The thunder of the guns and the immense clouds of smoke testified to the fierceness of the action.

During this time, Nelson, in the undress uniform of an admiral of the fleet but with his stars and decorations pinned on his breast, was walking on the quarterdeck with Captain Hardy and others.

Some forty feet above them on the mizzen top of the *Redoubtable*, one of the French sharpshooters looking through the swirling smoke saw the small figure below with the decorations on his chest, and took careful aim with his musket.

The ball struck Nelson's left shoulder and, mortally wounded, he fell to the deck.

As Captain Hardy bent over him Nelson spoke. 'They have done for me at last. My backbone is shot through.' He was carried below to the cockpit, his face covered with a handkerchief so that the crew would not be disheartened, and laid on a midshipman's berth. All around in noisome gloom, lit only by the dim light of candle lanthorns, lay scores of other wounded or dying men. It was obvious that Nelson's end was near. There was nothing the surgeon could do.

The battle raged on for another three hours. The *Redoubtable*, sandwiched between the *Victory* and the *Téméraire,* had been pounded into a virtual wreck. With 522 dead and wounded out of a total ship's company of 643, she had ceased fighting. Admiral Villeneuve's flagship, the *Bucentaure*, was in little better condition. The huge Spanish flagship, the *Santissima Trinidad*, had all her masts shot away and was rolling helplessly, as a succession of British ships poured in their broadsides. Both ships eventually hauled down their colours and surrendered.

The British ships had not come through undamaged. Many had suffered severely from the French broadsides as they approached the enemy line. Both the *Victory* and the *Royal Sovereign* were dismasted, but by three o'clock in the afternoon Hardy was able to tell Nelson that while fourteen or fifteen enemy ships had surrendered, not one British ship was lost.

And so the great sailor died with the knowledge of a brilliant victory. His last words were, 'Thank God – I have done my duty.'

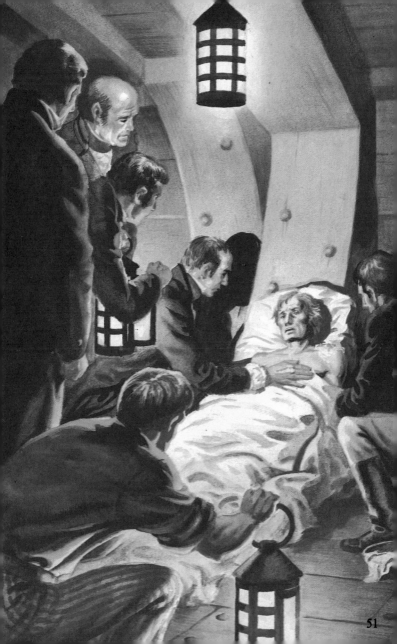

INDEX

page

Aboukir Bay 22-23
Agamemnon 12, 15, 18
America 10-11
Arctic 7
Atlantic Ocean 33, 43

Baltic 29
Blackwood, Captain 43
Brest 17
Bucentaure 45, 48, 50

Ça Ira 15
Cadiz 33, 43
Calvi 12
Cannon *see* Guns
Captain 18
Carronades 40, 48
Central America 10
Collingwood, Admiral 43, 44
Copenhagen 29
Corsica 12, 15

Denmark 28, 29, 31

East Indies 9
Egypt 22, 23, 24
Elba 16
English Channel 33
Euryalus 43

Foley, Captain 24
France 4, 12, 15, 17, 21, 22, 23, 24, 28, 29, 32, 33, 43, 44, 48, 49

page

George III 27
Goliath 24
Greece 23
Guns 36, 38-40, 44, 45, 48

Hamilton, Lady Emma 12, 26, 27, 43
Hamilton, Sir William 12, 26, 27
Hardy, Captain 49, 50, 51
Holland 29

Italy 21, 22, 27

Jervis, Admiral Sir John 15, 17, 21

King of Naples 27

Locker, Captain William 9
L' Orient 24, 25

Malta 23
Mediterranean 15, 21, 32
Merton 32

Naples 12, 27
Napoleon Bonaparte 4, 15, 21, 22, 24, 28, 32, 43
Nelson, Frances *see* Nesbit, Frances
Nelson, Horatio
  Boyhood 4, 6-7
  Death 4, 50-51
  Encounter with polar bear 6-7